RESIN BOOKMARK

Project Book

Learn how to create a
collection of resin crafts

5 projects inside

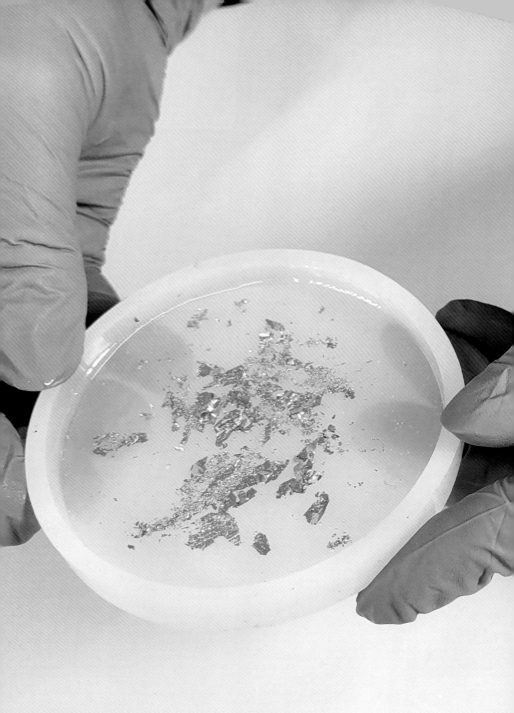

INTRODUCTION

Welcome to the world of Resin Craft!

This kit has been specifically designed for adult crafting only.

Learning a new skill is always exciting – we're here to help you get started. Anyone can learn how to make items with resin and with so many moulds, colours and designs to choose from, the only limit is your imagination.

Whether you're making a keepsake for yourself or as a gift for someone else, there's a great feeling of pride knowing that it's something you have created with your own hands. The good news is, most resin crafts cure fully in only a few days, which means you get to use, hang or wear your handmade item sooner than you might think!

Fancy a new bangle, bookmark or coaster? Well, you're in luck!

This kit provides everything you need to make your first resin craft bookmarks. There are four other makes with step-by-step instructions for you to try. You can decorate your creation to add your own personal touch with accessories such as dried flowers or glitter. Resin can also be coloured with dyes to create different effects.

Don't be disheartened if things don't work out the first time. Every skill takes time and effort to master. The most important thing is that you have fun and enjoy yourself. Think of how proud you'll feel when you have created your very own resin craft design.

Let's begin your resin craft journey.

KIT CONTENTS

WHAT'S INCLUDED:

- 20ml resin
- 20ml hardener
- Paper cup
- Bookmark mould
- Gold flakes
- Dried rose petals
- Tassel
- Mixing stick

(contains enough resin and decoration to make 2 bookmarks)

WHAT YOU'LL NEED:

- Protective gloves
- 2x measuring cups
- Small mixing bowl
- Newspaper or protective sheet

Ingredients:
Resin - Expoxy resin (CAS No.# 250968-38-6) AGE (CAS NO# 68609-97-2)
Defoamer (CAS No.# 87435-55-0)
Hardner. Polyamide (CAS No.# 63428-84-2) Expoxy Resin (CAS No.#25036-25-3).
Benzyl Alcohol (CAS No. #100-51-6)

WARNING!

ADULT USE ONLY

THIS CRAFT KIT IS DESIGNED SPECIFICALLY FOR ADULT CRAFTING ONLY.
Some people are allergic to resin and when exposed to uncured resin can get hives and swollen eyes. Keep resin away from children at all times. And keep projects that are still curing somewhere where they cannot get knocked over or played with. Resin is extremely sticky and will not come out of hair or off of skin easily. Wear protective gloves, safety goggles and old clothing. Avoid contact with skin and eyes. If serious eye irritation occurs or product is ingested, seek medical advice. Some contents may be flammable. Retain for future reference. Do in a well ventilated area with windows open.

WEAR NITRILE GLOVES TO PROTECT YOUR HANDS
The best safety gloves to wear when working with resin are nitrile or vinyl. Latex gloves are meant for medical practice and protect hands from viruses and bacteria, and are not made for chemical interactions.

HAVE GOOD VENTILATION IN YOUR ROOM FOR RESIN SAFETY
Many resin artists work with resin outside for safety. If you are working with resin indoors, you need to make sure there is proper air flow.

CONTINUE TO SAFELY VENTILATE AIR WHILE RESIN CURES
Each resin brand will have a different off gassing time and cure time. Read the directions and safety precautions included. Or go to the company's website for the safety data sheets.

Typically, full resin cure time is around 72 hours. During resin curing time, there is still resin in the air and to maintain resin safety, you will want to continue to safely ventilate the air until the resin piece or pieces are fully cured.

DON'T MIX RESIN WITH OTHER CHEMICALS IF IT GETS ON YOUR SKIN
In the case where some resin accidentally gets on your skin, do not try getting it off with alcohol, paint thinner or any other chemicals. Instead, try this safe, natural recipe to get resin safely off of skin:
·Pour about 1 tbsp. baking soda right into your hand
·Don't add any water
·Pour about 1 tbsp. of dish soap onto the baking soda
·Scrub your hands together over a sink
·Rinse your hands. Repeat if necessary

USE RESIN-ONLY DESIGNATED TOOLS
To keep resin from spreading to different tools and risk unanticipated exposure to skin, dedicate certain tools to resin only.

FOLLOW THE MIXING INSTRUCTIONS ON YOUR RESIN CONTAINER
Different brands and types of resin will tell you how much resin to mix and at what ratio. If you need to mix more resin than the brand suggests, then do it in batches. Mixing too much resin at a time could result in chemical reactions and the resin could heat up too much.

KEEP RESIN AWAY FROM PETS
Store resin up and away from pets at all times. This is especially important during the resin curing process because it's very sticky. Keep projects in a separate room where your pets will not be climbing or possibly knocking over your pieces.

ABOUT RESIN CRAFTING

RESIN

In recent years, resin crafts have become increasingly popular and are used in many craft makes, from jewellery to furniture. Resin is a liquid mixture that, when added to a hardener, sets hard and clear.

Epoxy resin is incredibly durable and resistant to wear and tear. Great right? It's easy to understand why so many people have taken an interest in it over the last few years. Many crafters use it to create amazing and beautiful things. It's so versatile and because it's clear, your creations can be decorated using all sorts of unique things.

So, let's make you an EPOXY MASTER!

MOULDS

You are not limited to the designs in this kit! There are many other moulds you can buy to add to your resin-making toolkit. The best moulds are silicone. These are easier to clean and remove your resin creations from. They can be found in craft stores both on the high street and online.

Want some new earrings? Go for it! A new display dish? Why not? Or maybe even a fancy paper weight! There are moulds for everything. Spend some time looking at the different choices and find something you'd love to make.

ACCESSORIES

Oh, the possibilities! The most popular are dried flowers, gold leaf and glitter. But that does not mean you are limited. The only limit is your imagination! You could add colourful buttons, scrap booking papers, crystals – truly, there are so many things, we simply could not list them all here.

As with the moulds, accessories can be found in craft stores both on the high street and online. Or, you can find things around your own home to use. It really depends on the size of your project and how you would like your resin craft to look.

TIPS & TECHNIQUES:

Fill your mould with water. Measuring the volume in this way will help to know how much resin to use and minimise wastage.

Mixing the resin and hardener together slowly will help to reduce air bubbles in the mixture. If bubbles persist, pop them before it sets.

Make sure you find a safe space to work that is unlikely to be disturbed as resin takes a while to set.

Working with resin can give you a headache. Make sure you are in a well ventilated room.
A silicone mat is best to help protect your surfaces, however, newspaper or baking paper will do just fine.

If you use a plastic mould, you will need a mould release spray to help remove the resin. Also, check all moulds are dust free using tape or washing them with warm soapy water. Your mould MUST be bone dry before use!

Make sure you have everything you need to hand! Once you start mixing your resin it will start to cure.

Do not leave food or drinks near your work area. Resin is a toxic chemical!

WEAR GLOVES!

Cover your completed design. An empty plastic tub placed upside down and over your project will do the trick. The last thing you want is something to ruin all your hard work!

BOUQUET BOOKMARK

BOUQUET BOOKMARK

Leave your mark on your favourite book with this beautiful floral bookmark. This resin craft kit includes the ingredients you need, along with this step by step guide. So, let's go!

KIT CONTAINS

· 20ml resin
· 20ml hardener
· Bookmark mould
· Gold flakes
· Dried rose petals
· Tassel
· Mixing stick
(contains enough resin
and decoration to make
2 bookmarks)

YOU WILL NEED

· Gloves
· 2 x measuring cups
· Small mixing bowl
· Newspaper or
protective sheet

METHOD

1. Set up your working area - you will need a clear space as working with resin can be messy. It's a good idea to put down newspaper or a sheet to protect your working area. Always wear gloves when working with resin.

2. Pour water into the mould and then measure how much water it holds. This will tell you approximately how much resin mixture you need for the mould and will reduce wasting resin.

3. Use the dried rose petals and gold flakes to distribute into the mould in the desired design. (Make sure the decoration does not sit higher than the top of the mould so the resin will cover it fully.)

4. You can move the decorative pieces around until you are happy with the layout of design.

5. Resin and hardener need to be mixed at a ratio of 1:1

6. Take the total amount of water that you measured in your mould and measure out half that amount of resin in one measuring cup and half that amount of hardener into another measuring cup. Approximately 10ml resin & 10ml hardener per bookmark.

7. Pour these into a clean bowl together. Make sure to waste as little as possible when transferring from the measuring cups to the bowl.

8. Mix the two together for 2 mins very slowly to remove streaks and avoid creating air bubbles.

9. Once you can see all the streaks have been eliminated you can pour the mixture into the mould covering the decoration and filling the mould to the top.

10. Then let it set. For best results leave for 24 hours.

11. Once set, gently remove the mould by peeling it from the resin.

12. Thread your tassel through the hole in the top of the bookmark.

13. Your new bookmark is now ready to use.

Well Done!

AUTUMN

MUSHROOM

OUR CONNECTION WITH NATURE

"...and I live in a world where there are Octobers."
— L.M. Montgomery, *Anne of Green Gables (1908)*

Autumn is my favourite season and what better way to honour it than by embroidering fungi. The mushroom is widely known and used in cultures all over the world; in folklore, they are often used for medicine, food and spiritual reasons. They symbolise power, abundance, longevity, rebirth, harmony...

Mushrooms have a symbiotic connection to the trees and plants around them and are often the last standing remains of... that we have a connection with something... work that is always present, but usually unseen. Mushrooms represent the link between people and the Earth. My curiosity... I spot mushrooms while exploring outside, and whenever I think of autumn, fungi are conjured up in my mind...

This embroidery design was inspired by the Boletes mushroom family, of which there are over one-hundred different species... favourite parts of this pattern is... have fun blending the colours, and finding out how the stitches sit together... other. I designed this pattern so that if you don't place your stitches in exactly... me, and the overall effect will still be pretty much the same. So don't be afraid... these two mushrooms – there is lots of room for happy mistakes! Feel free... and enjoy the repetitive nature of the stitching.

10   62

Rich
me,

the
ere is a
of the
ked when
nages of

over
can
each
lace as
ering
flow

NOTES

Use the space below to make your own personal notes on the previous project to help when you come back to make it again!

HOME IS WHERE
THE HEART IS

HOME IS WHERE THE HEART IS

Add a little heart to your home with this cute resin wall sign.

EQUIPMENT
- Mixing stick
- Gloves
- 2 x measuring cups
- Small mixing bowl
- Newspaper or protective sheet
- Decorative sign mould (HOME)

YOU WILL NEED
- Resin
- Hardener
- Flowers

METHOD

1. Set up your working area – you will need a clear space as working with resin can be messy. It's a good idea to put down newspapers or sheets to protect your working area. Always wear gloves when working with resin.

2. Fill the mould with water, then measure how much water it holds. Divide this amount by 2 and that will be approximately the amount of hardener and resin you need for the mould.

3. Add your flowers, in the arrangement of your choice, into your sign mould.

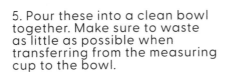

4. Measure out the resin and hardener into the mixing cups.

5. Pour these into a clean bowl together. Make sure to waste as little as possible when transferring from the measuring cup to the bowl.

6. Mix together for 2 mins very slowly to remove streaks and avoid creating air bubbles.

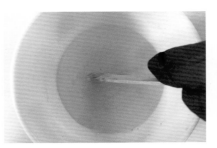

7. Once you can see all the streaks have been eliminated you can pour the mixture into the mould, filling the mould to the top.

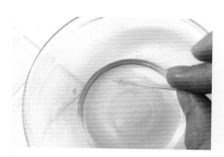

8. Leave to set for at least 24hrs before removing from the mould.

9. Once set this will be ready to display proudly in your home or as a gift for someone else.

Congratulations! You now have a beautiful decorative sign to hang or give as a gift.

NOTES

Use the space below to make your own personal notes on the
previous project to help when you come back to make it again!

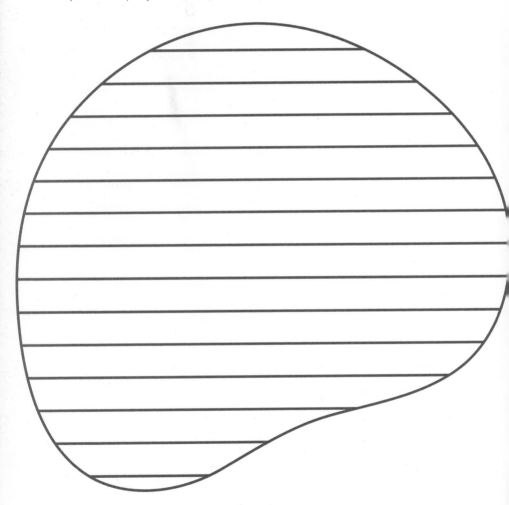

GLITTER
BANGLE

GLITTER BANGLE

Bring a personal touch to your jewellery by creating your own bangle! Pick the colours that suit you, or even give as a gift to a loved one!

EQUIPMENT
· Pipette
· Gloves
· 2 x measuring cups
· Small mixing bowl
· Cocktail stick
· Newspaper or protective sheet.
· Silicone bangle mould
· Mixing stick

YOU WILL NEED
· Resin
· Hardener
· Glitter

METHOD

1. Set up your working area, you will need a clear space as working with resin can be messy. It's a good idea to put down newspapers or sheets to protect your working area. Always wear gloves when working with resin.

2. Fill the mould with water, then measure how much water it holds. Divide this amount by 2 and that will be approximately the amount of hardener and resin you need for the mould.

3. Measure out the resin and hardener into the mixing cups.

4. Pour these into a clean bowl together. Make sure to waste as little as possible when transferring from the measuring cup to the bowl.

5. Mix the two together for 2 mins very slowly to remove streaks and avoid creating air bubbles.

6. Pour some glitter into your mixture and mix using your wooden stick.

7. Once stirred, use your pipette to fill your mould and clean around the edges using the stick.

8. Leave to set for at least 24hrs
before removing from the mould.

9. Once set this will be ready
to wear or give as a gift for
someone else.

And there you have it!

NOTES

Use the space below to make your own personal notes on the
previous project to help when you come back to make it again!

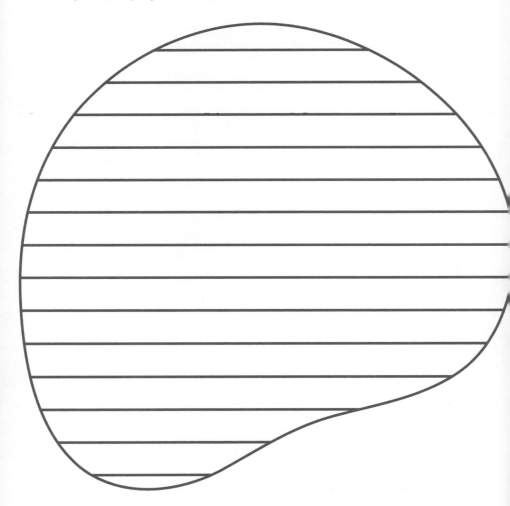

ALPHABET KEYRING

ALPHABET KEYRING

Personalise your keys with this beautiful dried flower keyring!
Experiment with different colours, flowers and fruits. Perfectly
personal for you or a friend.

EQUIPMENT

· Gloves
· 2 x measuring
cups
· Small mixing bowl
· Cocktail stick
· Newspaper or
protective sheet
· Letter mould
· Mixing stick

YOU WILL NEED

· Resin
· Hardener
· 1 x coloured mica
powder
· Dried flowers
· Dried fruit

METHOD

1. Set up your working area - you will need a clear space as working with resin can be messy. It's a good idea to put down newspapers or sheets to protect your working area. Always wear gloves when working with resin.

2. Fill the mould with water, then measure how much water it holds. Divide this amount by 2 and that will be approximately the amount of hardener and resin you need for the mould.

3. In your mould, add in the dried flowers and fruit.
Arrange these in the design you would like, but make sure they don't protrude over the top of the mould.

4. Measure out the resin and hardener into the mixing cups.

5. Pour these into a clean bowl together. Make sure to waste as little as possible when transferring from the measuring cup to the bowl.

6. Mix the two together for 2 mins very slowly to remove streaks and avoid creating air bubbles.

7. Pour the resin evenly into the mould.

8. Use a cocktail stick to swirl in gold mica powder colouring.

9. Leave to set for 24hrs before removing from the mould.

10. Once removed from the mould screw in the keyring attachment.

What a beautiful gift! Or maybe you're going to keep this one to show off to your friends.

NOTES

Use the space below to make your own personal notes on the previous project to help when you come back to make it again!

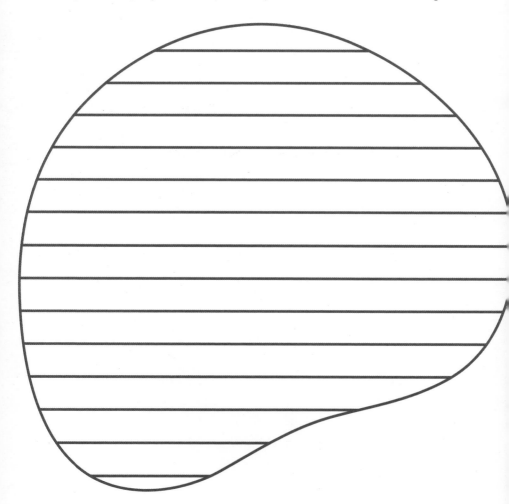

FLOWER POWER

FLOWER POWER

Bring the outside in with these cute floral coasters! Choose your flowers, whether they are dainty daisies or perfect pansies, there's a design for you.

EQUIPMENT

· Gloves
· 2 x measuring cups
· Small mixing bowl
· Newspaper or protective sheet
· Round coaster mould
· Mixing stick

YOU WILL NEED

· Resin
· Hardener
· Dried flowers

METHOD

1. Set up your working area - you will need a clear space as working with resin can be messy. It's a good idea to put down newspapers or sheets to protect your working area. Always wear gloves when working with resin.

2. Fill the mould with water, then measure how much water it holds. Divide this amount by 2 and that will be the amount of hardener and resin you need for the mould.

3. In your mould, add in the dried flowers facing down so when removed the bottom will become the top. Arrange these in the design you would like, but make sure they do not protrude over the top of the mould.

4. Measure out the resin and hardener into the mixing cups.

5. Pour these into a clean bowl together. Make sure to waste as little as possible when transferring from the measuring cup to the bowl.

6. Mix the two together for 2 mins very slowly to remove streaks and avoid creating air bubbles.

7. Pour the resin evenly into the mould.

8. Leave to set for 24hrs.

9. Remove from the mould when fully set.

Great job! Well done!

NOTES

Use the space below to make your own personal notes on the previous project to help when you come back to make it again!

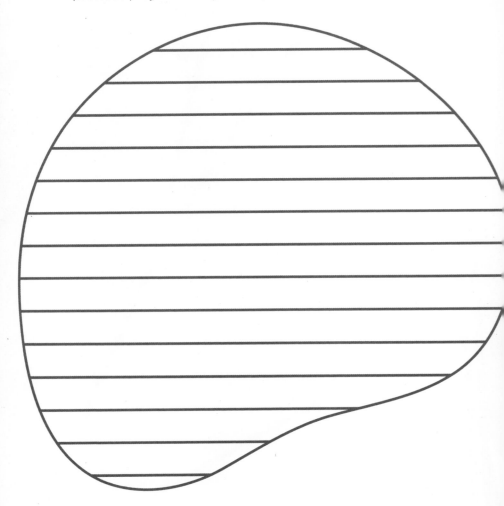